On Stage

by Theresa Bryson

She is a musician.

She is playing the violin.

She is on stage.

3

He is an acrobat.

He is leaping through a hoop.

He is on stage, too.

She is a singer.

She sings on stage.

She is an actor.

She acts on stage.

He is a clown.

He is wearing a red nose.

He is on stage.

He is a magician.

He is doing a trick.

He is on stage, too.

He is a dancer.

He is jumping in the air.

He dances on stage.

They are on stage.
They are dancers, too!